sundance

LITTLE READER
TWIN TEXTS

W9-BEH-974

My Heroes

Written by Julia Stanton
Illustrated by Carol Daniel

Content Strand: America
Focus: Heroes

Every Sunday, Uncle Jimmy
came for dinner.
He always played checkers
with Andy and me.

Sometimes Andy won.
Sometimes I won.

It was fun to play
with Uncle Jimmy.

One day, Uncle Jimmy fell
and hurt his leg.

He had to go
to the hospital.

Uncle Jimmy couldn't
come to our house
on Sundays anymore.

We missed him.

After Uncle Jimmy got
home from the hospital,
he was sad.
It was hard for him
to get around.

We went to see him
every day.
But he didn't even want
to play checkers with us.

He just sat in his chair.
We couldn't cheer him up.

Then Andy and I remembered that Uncle Jimmy loved parrots.

He always told us stories about the parrot he used to have.

So we decided to buy him another one.

Maybe that would cheer him up.

We gave the parrot
to Uncle Jimmy.

It cheered him up
right away!

He called us his heroes.

He decided to call
his parrot Rudy.

The "Ru" comes from
Ruth—that's me.
And the rest comes from
Andy.

Now Uncle Jimmy
has his checkers ready
when we visit.

And Rudy always likes
to see us, too!